This book is dedicated to my son, R. L. Van Flimen

and my husband, Master Gil Van Flimen.

Thank you for your support.

Without you, this book would never come to light.

How to choose the attractions that you would like to visit with your toddler in Cyprus?

Introduction

We're a family of three, two adults and a curious 3 year old boy who enjoys playgrounds, Luna parks, adventure parks, and parks where there are animals. All of Cyprus looks like paradise from his eyes.

It was his 3rd birthday week, I chose Cyprus because the people there like kids and are relatively very friendly! The common foods there are pastas, fried potatoes and fish, all things that my son enjoys.

Below, you'll find a list of all the attractions that have the potential to be interesting for my family within Cyprus;

Larnaca is the ancient city of Cyprus, there is evidence of inhabitance in the area from over 6,000 years ago. As a family, you have the ability to stay in Larnaca for several holidays. While you can enjoy the wonderful hotels, the successful restaurants, there's also the beach promenade, known as Finikoudes, that is decorated with palm trees and wonderful attractions for the whole family that surrounds Larnaca.

Finikoudes Beach

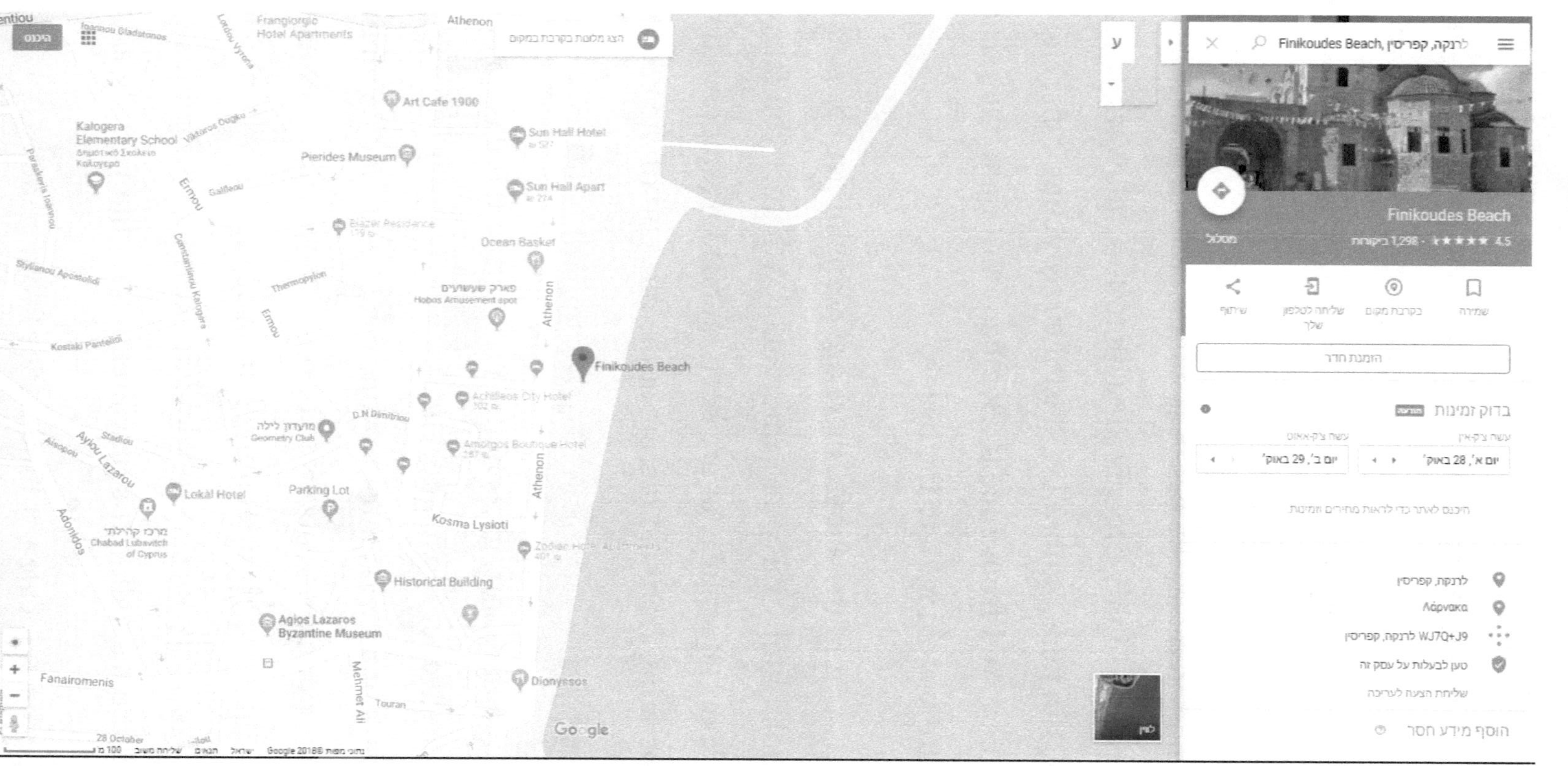
fxentiou
Athenon
Frangiorgio Hotel Apartments
Ioannou Gladstonos
Ladou Vyrota
Art Cafe 1900
Kalogera Elementary School
Δημοτικό Σχολείο Καλογραφού
Pierides Museum
Sun Hall Hotel
Sun Hall Apart
Galileou
Ermou
Paraskevis Ioannou
Brazier Residence
Ocean Basket
Stylianou Apostolidi
Thermopylion
Constantinou Kalogera
Ermou
פארק שעשועים
Hobos Amusement spot
Athenon
Kostaki Pantelidi
Finikoudes Beach
Achilleos City Hotel
Stadiou
Aylou Lazarou
Alsopou
D.N Dimitriou
מועדון לילה
Geometry Club
Amorgos Boutique Hotel
Athenon
Lokal Hotel
Parking Lot
Adonidos
מרכז קהילתי
Chabad Lubavitch of Cyprus
Kosma Lysioti
Zodiac Hotel All
Historical Building
Agios Lazaros Byzantine Museum
Mehmet Ali
Fanairomenis
Dionyssos
Touran
28 October
Google
נתוני מפה Google 2018©
100 מ'
הצג מסעות בקרבת במקום
לרנקה, קפריסין
Finikoudes Beach,
Finikoudes Beach
1,298 ביקורות · ★★★★★ 4.5
מסלול
שיתוף
שליחה לטלפון שלך
בקרבת מקום
שמירה
הזמנת חדר
בדוק זמינות
עשרה צ'ק-אין
עשרה צ'ק-אאוט
יום א', 28 באוק'
יום ב', 29 באוק'
היכנס לאתר כדי לראות מחירים זמינות
לרנקת, קפריסין
Λάρνακα
J9+WJ7Q לרנקה, קפריסין
טען לבעלות על עסק זה
שליחת הצעה לעריכה
הוסף מידע חסר

This one can be considered an obvious choice, and for good reason! Backed by a pretty palm tree lined promenade, and flanked by a marina and pier on one end, a medieval castle on the other, the water there is shallow and cam, with the area being packed with things to do.

First and foremost, the beach is abundant with necessities and luxuries and highly organized, with toilets, showers, changing rooms, sun beds, umbrellas, dustbins, recycling bins, and a beach bar. And from June to October, until 6pm, there is a lifeguard watching over the beach.

But, apart from the above, there are heaps of activities to keep the whole family busy and entertained, whether you fancy a water sport adventure, or are keen on heading out on a boat trip operating from the marina at the one end of the beach strip.

Kids love the short, glass bottom rides, and there is no need to book in advance! Just take a walk down the pier and choose the ride that appeals most to you. When you fancy a nibble, there are countless options to choose from, with cafes and restaurants side by side, ice cream shops and kiosks at what seem like every turn. And when the kids fancy a game on dry land, there's a children's play area within the vicinity as well!

This beach is located at Finikoudes Promenade.

Municipal Gardens

Located in a large city triangle, formed by Afxentiou, Kiouppis, and Pierides streets, the Municipal Gardens are extensive grounds that incorporate the Municipal Theatre, Library, and Museum of Natural History, as well as a children's playground with two areas of equipment and toys for use of all ages.

The playground and library are free of charge to enjoy, whilst the theatre hosts a variety of cultural performances on an almost daily basis with varying ticket fees. The museum incurs a nominal fee and showcases a variety of animals, marine life, birds, shells, and insects.

The *Statue of Liberty* is situated right in front of the library, and the artwork, *The Blare of Peace*, is displayed in front of the Municipal Theatre.

There is even a marble statue of the philosopher *Zanon of Kition* erected opposite of the gardens dating back from the 1920's.

Agios Georgiou

Kontou Playground

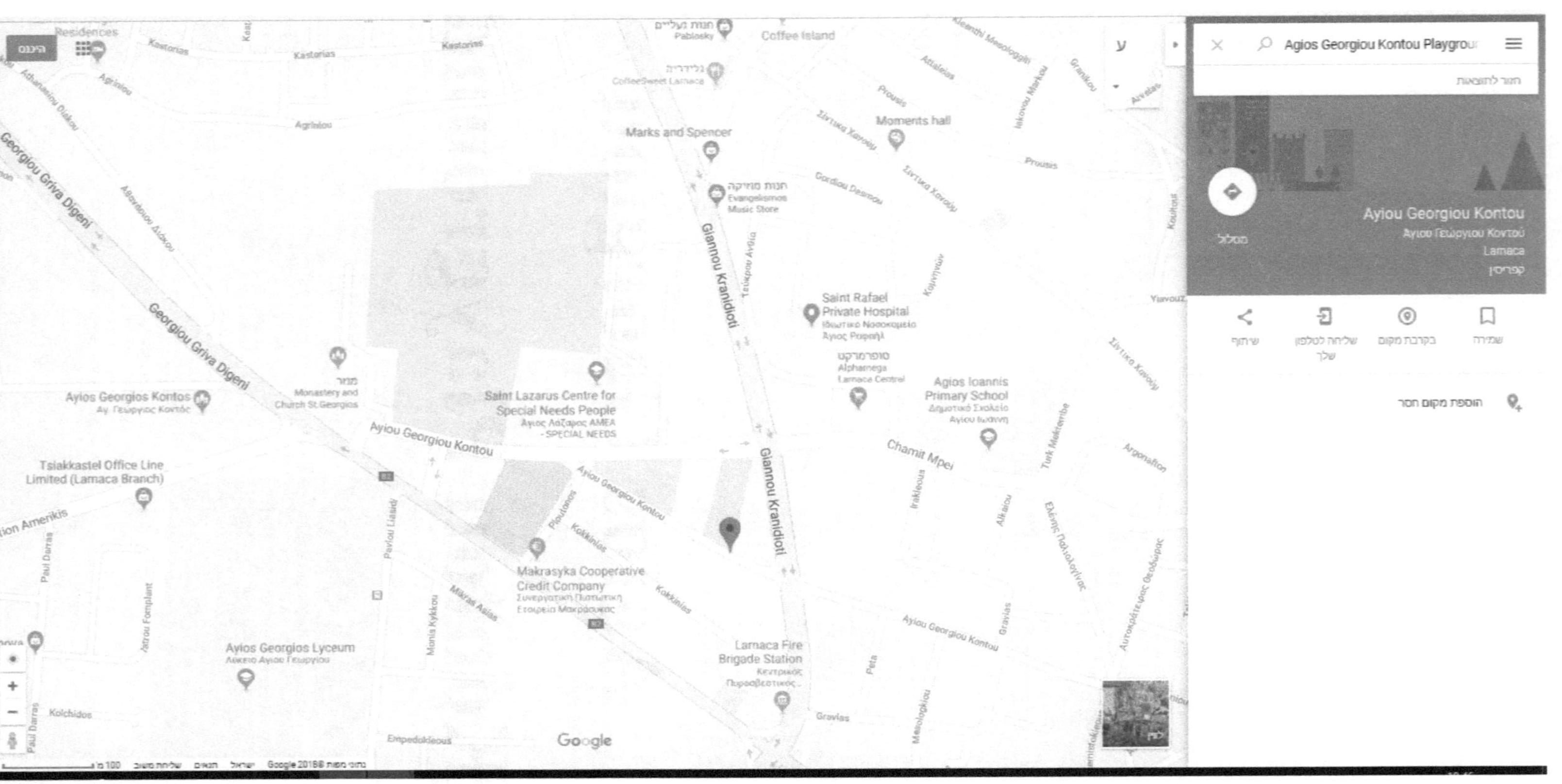

Agios Georgiou Kontou Playgrou
חזור לתוצאות
Ayiou Georgiou Kontou
Αγίου Γεωργίου Κοντού
Larnaca
קפריסין
מסלול
שיתוף
בקרבת מקום
שליחה לטלפון שלך
שמירה
הוספת מקום חסר
Residences
היכנס
Coffee Island
Pablosky
CoffeeSweet Larnaca
Moments hall
Marks and Spencer
Evangelismos Music Store
Georgiou Griva Digeni
Saint Rafael Private Hospital
Ιδιωτικό Νοσοκομείο Άγιος Ραφαήλ
Alphamega Larnaca Central
Agios Ioannis Primary School
Δημοτικό Σχολείο Αγίου Ιωάννη
Ayios Georgios Kontos
Αγ. Γεώργιος Κοντός
Monastery and Church St.Georgios
Saint Lazarus Centre for Special Needs People
Άγιος Λάζαρος ΑΜΕΑ - SPECIAL NEEDS
Giannou Kranidioti
Chamit Mpei
Ayiou Georgiou Kontou
Tsiakkastel Office Line Limited (Larnaca Branch)
Polition Amerikis
Paul Darras
Makrasyka Cooperative Credit Company
Συνεργατική Πιστωτική Εταιρεία Μακράσυκας
Larnaca Fire Brigade Station
Κεντρικός Πυροσβεστικός
Ayios Georgios Lyceum
Λύκειο Άγιος Γεώργιος
Kolchidos
Empedokleous
Google
100 מ׳
Google 2018 נתוני מפות

An outdoor playground for children in Cyprus should be one of the main reasons for parents to consciously choose to spend their day out in the sun. And with that, the best medicine for kids to get rid of that nasty old, to lose energy for a wonderful nights rest. In order to be sure, however, that all these conditions are met, parents should be sure they've spent the right amount of time outside, in the fresh air. If you live in Larnaka, or are just passing through, and you've got your children with you, be sure to keep an eye out for the playground next to Agios Georgiou Kontou church, you don't want to miss out, as it's a wonderful place!

The playground is decently big in size, operating over an artificial grass, and everyone is sure to find something to do – from babies to parents – you are all bound to enjoy the day out. The playground is bordered by fencing and has a large parking lot, making it easy and accessible for all.

Parents can find swings, a roundabout, climbing areas, and slides all toddler friendly, and toddler proofed. For bigger children, there are also swings, climbing structures, and even a zip line. One of the best things about this playground, without a doubt, is that right to the side of it, there are three mini football fields, and one basketball or tennis field. If you are interested in playing with your bigger kids by participating in any of these games, be prepared to bring some sport equipment with you.

There is plenty of space to run, ride the bicycle or scooter, or skate on the pathways that cross the sports fields.

At Agios Georgiou Kontou playground, there is a coffee shop where you can find a snack for your hungry ones. Next to the playground, you'll find more than 4 tables that gives you plenty ideas for a budget birthday party. It is a wonderful idea that from time to time, to invite your children's friends and gather for a nice play, even if there is no special occasion.

Agios Georgiou Kontou is the perfect place in Larnaca, for parents to enjoy their kids while they play and run around in the fresh air, to practice a sport or to celebrate a birthday for any age!

Fun Factory

Opening hours:

Summer hours:

Every day: 10:00 – 22:00

Starting from September:

Monday – Friday: 10:00 – 21:00

Friday – Sunday: 10:00 -22: 00

Entrance fee: 4.50 Euro per child

Address: 2 Yiannou Kranidioti Ave., Larnaka Showroom 1, Cyprus

Phone no: +357 70 004 095

E-mail: funfactorylarnaca@hotmail.com

Web page: https://www.facebook.com/funfactory.larnaca

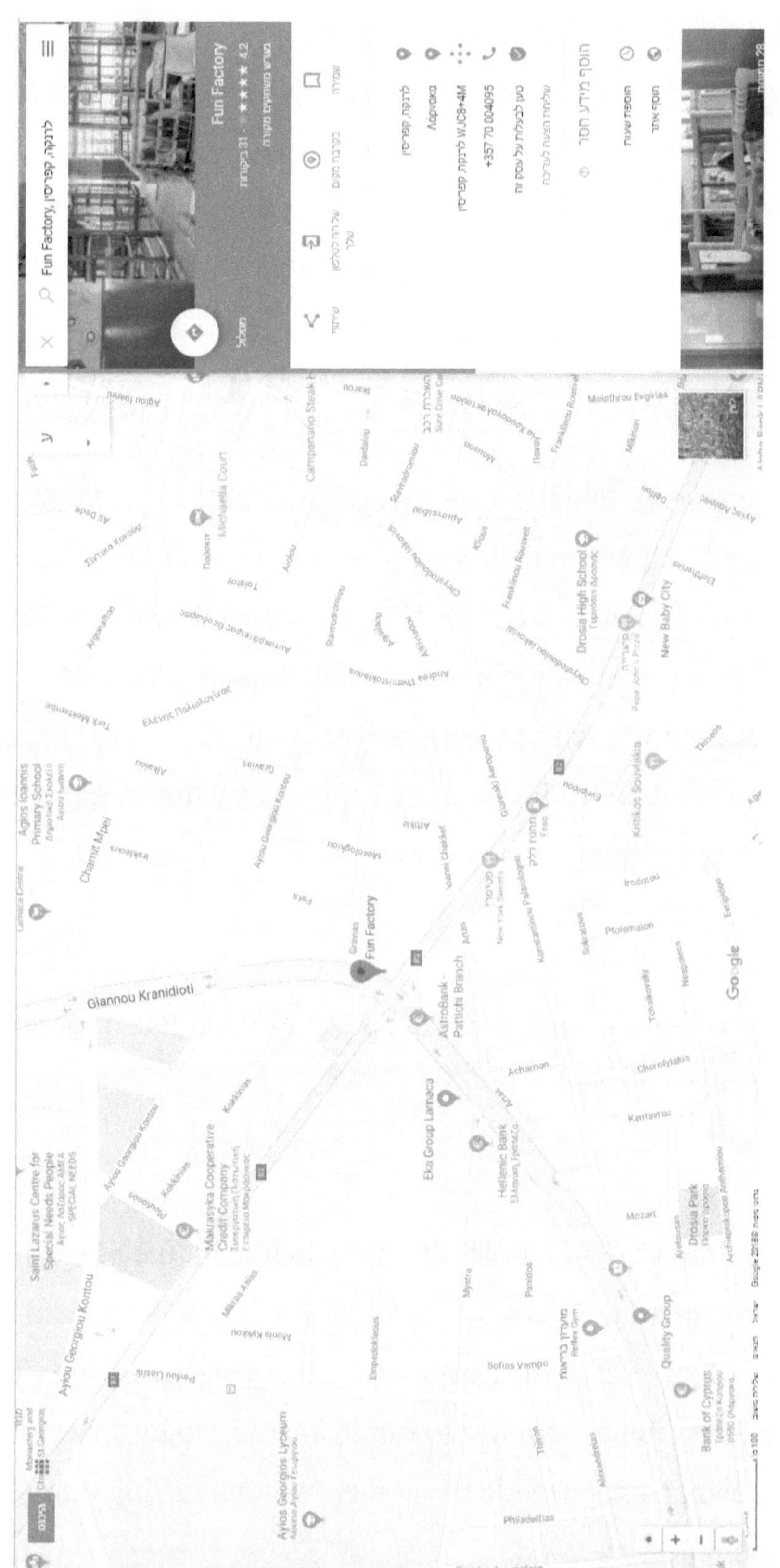

Fun Factory is a place where "kids fun in Cyprus" feels good every single time we visit, and now have had the opportunity to go again and discover a completely new playground under new management we are ready to share with our readers. We loved the new Fun Factory playground in Lamaka with all new games and additions, it's spacious, big, and full of fun!

We personally like it because parents are able to sit at any table and still watch their kids play, all the while drinking a nice cup of coffee! We love the interest that they are showing to the toddlers area, which is safe and harbors plenty of interesting toys. All of the employees that take care of children are qualified, love kids, and are happy every time they're able to entertain them.

The new Fun Factory playground brings upon lots of new games for children!

For children 1-3 years old, there is a ball pool, the biggest pleasure of all toddlers, a new kitchen to enjoy household chores, lots of drawing activities for everyone, and more. It is a fantastic, fun experience to run in a large, sunny space up and down, from one side to another, without having mum look for them every second.

For children 4-12, there is a twisted blue slide and yellow rocket connected to the new spider game, many structures for climbing, a big trampoline, a small basketball court where they can practice sportive skills, a new multitasking game with lots of surprises and a slide.

Fun Factory also takes care of what children eat, having it's own kitchen, children and parents would definitely enjoy the new a la carte menu, with a great variety of foods to satisfy all tastes with a separate, special menu for children. Some healthy choices we will mention are, chicken souvlaki, pork chop, salmon steak, tuna wrap, and goat cheese salad.

Upstairs, there's another play area which can be entirely separated from the one below creating a place only for your guests – the ideal private party.

One last thing I'd like to note, is the outdoor terrace, elegant with a nice view ideal for a relaxing mum's meeting.

So, Fun Factory, here we come! Thank you for the excellent service, quality, opening hours, and prices!

Ciokoland

Opening hours:

Mon - Fri: Summer 17:00 – 22:00 – Winter 16:00 -22:00

Sat - Sun: Summer 16:00 – 22:00 - Winter 11:00 – 22:00

Entrance fee: 3.00 euro

Address: Pelloponisou Street and Potamou Indou Street no. 1, 6301 Larnaca, Cyprus

Web page: http://ciokoland.com/

Phone no: +357 24 819022

This place is truly amazing. It has a small area for the little ones where they can climb, crawl, and do essentially whatever they want, but is very clean and tidy while their mothers can drink nice hot chocolates or soothing coffees with chocolate candies attached. It is all about chocolate here.

What I've liked most was the brand new carousel, adorned with so many lights and colors, and the train for the kids, as well as all the new machines are just clean and visually pleasing. There is a small playground with a slide and balls for anyone looking to waste a little energy on fun. Let's not forget the guns that shoot balls, which brought value to the place.

Ciokoland is adjacent to the K Cineplex Larnaca, so it is easy to visit here for a nice afternoon, trying also the cinema, bowling, or restaurants. It's very good for those whose children are different in ages and expectations, as there's plenty of things to do for everyone.

Do not forget to try at least one of the chocolate candies, they're truly fantastic!

Lucky Star Park,

Arradippou

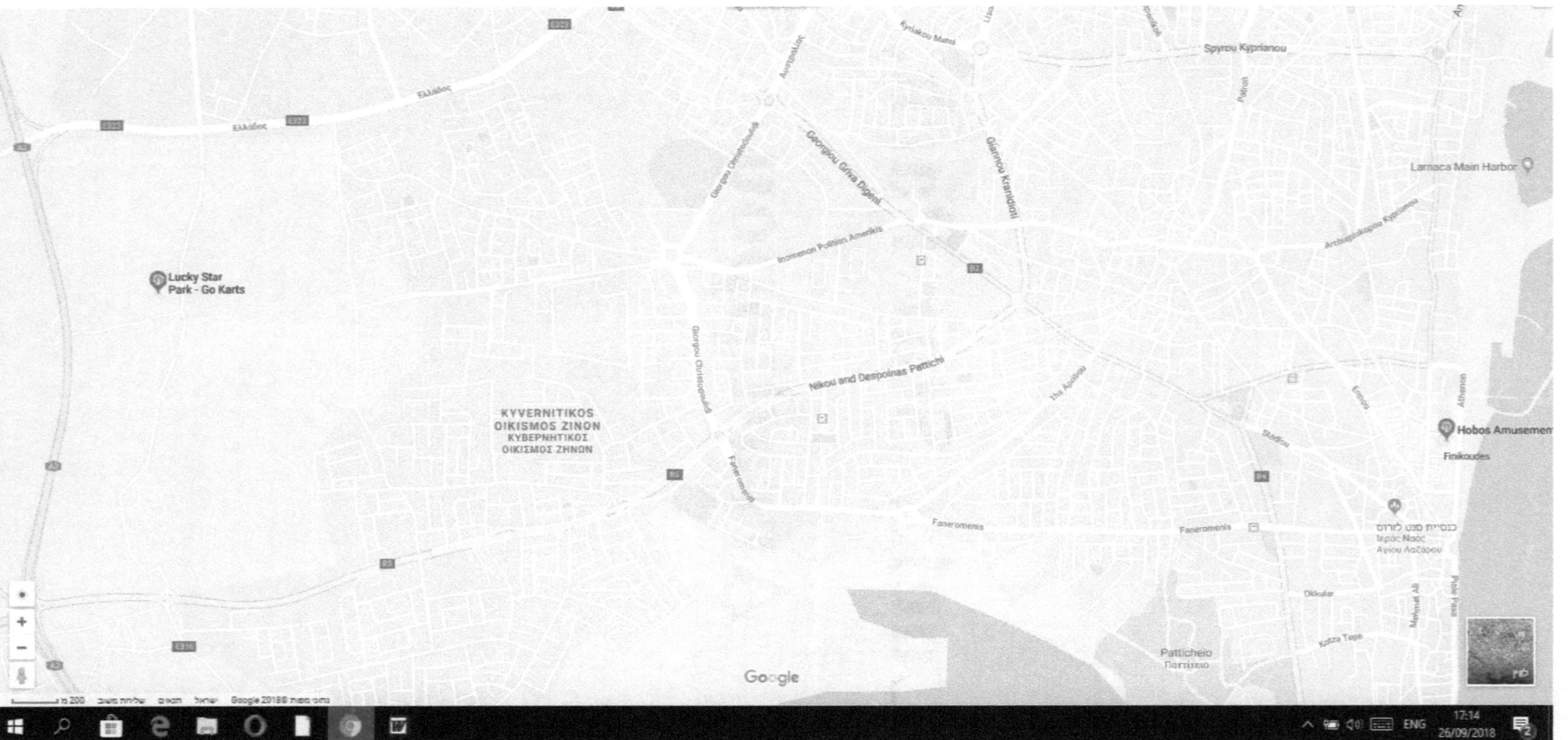

Spyrou Kyprianou
Kyriakou Matsi
Patron
Ellados
Larnaca Main Harbor
Georgiou Griva Digeni
Giannou Kranidioti
Archiepiskopou Kyprianou
Lucky Star
Park - Go Karts
Iromenon Pushion Amerikis
Giorgou Christodoulou
Giorgou Christodoulou
Nikou and Despoinas Pattichi
Ths Aphron
Athenon
KYVERNITIKOS
OIKISMOS ZINON
ΚΥΒΕΡΝΗΤΙΚΟΣ
ΟΙΚΙΣΜΟΣ ΖΗΝΩΝ
Hobos Amusement
Finikoudes
Faneromenis
Faneromenis
Faneromenis
Erimou
Ieróc Naóc
Agiou Lazarou
Dikular
Mehmet Ali
Kutza Tepe
Pisie Pasa
Patticheio
Google
1:200
Google 2018
17:14
26/09/2018
ENG

Lucky Star Park is a huge complex with such a large variety of amusements and activities that everyone is certain to have a good time. One day really isn't enough to try out all the attractions within the park.

Contact data

Phone +357 24 534400
E-mail: info@luckystarpark.co
Website: www.luckystarpark.com.cy

Address

Agiou Sergiou & Vanchou 50, 7100 Aradippu, Larnaca, Cyprus

Working hours

Monday — Sunday (except Tuesday):
16:00 — 00:00
Tuesday: day off

Go Kart advance bookings of 4 people opening time: any

There is a wide variety of entertainment available for children of all ages.

Bumper Cars – This type of entertainment, racing cars and carts, is not only popular with children, but adults as well. There is a special mini track for kids and a larger track for the adults.

Motorcycle Racing – Both, adults and children, can race on the carting track, whereas only children may ride on the motorcycle course. This attraction imitates a real race, and the participants are fully instructed beforehand.

Bumper Boats – Another form of carting, however, this time, on water! Instead of a track, there is a pool, and the young captains are in charge of special bumper boats.

Train Safari – Both children and parents will enjoy a ride all over the park on a little train decorated with illustrations of animals.

Roller coasters – This attraction promises a much more exciting ride. Don't forget to fasten your seat belts as the carriages change direction unexpectedly and move along at high speeds.

Carousels – The park has a musical carousel for the little ones to transport them into a magical world.

Monorail – This attraction gives the kids a bird's eye view of the whole park, and an opportunity to make friends along the way with fellow travelers.

Antique cars – In addition to racing cars, motorcycles, and trains, the children have the opportunity as well to get acquainted with antique cars. The children can take a photo with this unique mode of transport as a memento.

Trambolino – Children from 2-14 will enjoy this attraction where they can spend the whole day on the Trambolino.

Lucky Games – This attraction is for dexterous and lucky players. Here, the children can demonstrate their skills and leadership abilities, winning something if they're lucky.

Together with friends, they can also play billiard, football, air hockey, and video games, while the younger children also have a wide selection of toys to play with.

Camel Park, Mazotos

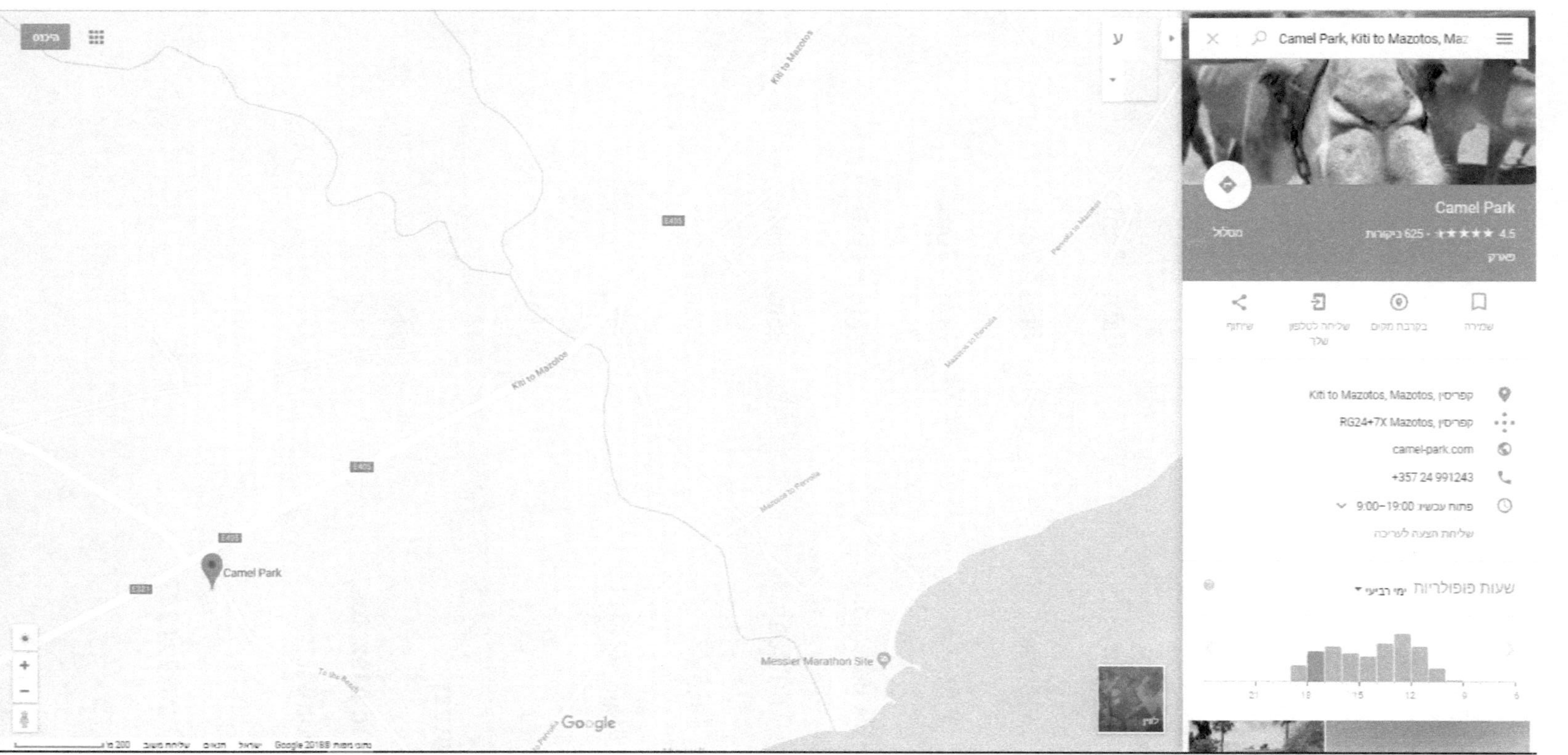

היכנס
Camel Park, Kiti to Mazotos, Maz
Camel Park
4.5 ★★★★★ · 625 ניקורות
פארק
מסלול
שמירה
בקרבת מקום
שליחה לטלפון שלך
שיתוף
Kiti to Mazotos, Mazotos, קפריסין
RG24+7X Mazotos, קפריסין
camel-park.com
+357 24 991243
פתוח עכשיו · 9:00–19:00
שליחת הצעה לעריכה
שעות פופולריות · ימי רביעי
Kiti to Mazotos
Kiti to Mazotos
Mazotos to Pervolia
Pervolia to Mazotos
Mazotos to Pervolia
Camel Park
Messier Marathon Site
To the Beach
Google
Google 2018

Recommended Duration

4 hours

Hours

Sunday	9am - 7pm
Monday	9am - 7pm
Tuesday	9am - 7pm
Wednesday	9am - 7pm
Thursday	9am - 7pm
Friday	9am - 7pm
Saturday	9am - 7pm

Contact

Kiti to Mazotos,

Mazotos,

Cyprus

+357 24 991243

Parking

Lot parking available

Prices:

Adult Entrance Fee 4 Euros*

Child Entrance Fee 3 Euros*

Adult Camel Ride 10 Euros*

The Camel Park at Mazotos is conveniently location, standing about 15 minutes away from the Larnaca Airport, and centrally located between Larnaca, Limassol, and Nicosia. As you walk into the park, you will understand that this is truly a wonderful day out for the family. There are play areas for children, games, and so much more. The Camel Park is a place where all have the ability to learn about other animals that live there, such as ostriches, goats, deer, ponies, wallabies, lamas, turtles, fish, many variations of bird, and much more.

The Camel Park also offers the great opportunity of riding a camel around the park, along with having a great memorable picture taken. You can also purchase sacks of food to feed the animals close up.

There is also a great play area for children, from bull riding games, to 5D cinema for the little ones, as well as play rides to amuse them. Walking around the park, you can take in all the camels, all on a pleasant stroll.

In the summer, we open up our swimming pool area, offering refreshments, snacks, and drinks hot and cold. Be prepared to stay a while at the swimming pool area surrounded by greenery, as it offers a great afternoon out.

We also cater for lunch and dinner in our restaurant area, presenting meals such as salads, side dishes, pizzas, pastas, snacks, burgers, wraps, grilled, sea food, beverages and desserts.

Camel Ride – Take a unique safari ride through the countryside on one of our friendly camels. This is our biggest attraction, and for good reason, and an experience you won't find in many places around the world! The exciting ride lasts about 10-15 minutes and is something that shouldn't be missed! Prices are 7 euro for kids, 10 for adults. Entrance fees of 3 and 4 euro's will be deducted from this price. Price also includes use of the pool!

Swimming Pool – What better way to relax after your camel ride? Summer days in Cyprus can get excessively hot, but not to worry, we've got just the solution. Our swimming pool is surrounded by plenty greenery, making it a cool paradise on those hot summer days. There is a small kids pool, near the main one, for our young guests as well!

Kids Area – In the kids area, there is a 5D cinema, bumper cars, and a miniature train ride, amongst others, we have some activities free of charge, such as swings and the mirror room! There are plenty of benches that adults can sit back and relax. All whilst their kids enjoy their time playing. Additionally, there is an indoor game area, with coin operated rides.

Feeding the animals – You can feed the goats with carob, which you can buy at the entrance for 0.5 Euro. I bought 2 bags for me an my 3 year old son. At first, he was very afraid of the goats that came to eat, but after seeing how brave I was, he fed them and enjoyed it very much, was even disappointed when we had no carobs to feed them.

Little zoo – We came in the spring, as is recommended. The picklocks stole the show for all the animals, they made plenty of noise, waved their big tails, opening them up. My son thought they'd wanted candy from their mother, which was why they were doing it. Besides the picklocks, however, there were plenty of other animals as well.

There's even a pony ride!

We stayed all day long, and loved it immensely. We drove from Limassol specifically for it, don't miss it, especially if you're in Larnaca.

In the next pages, you'll see several photos from our trip:

My husband photographed me with the camel before I sneezed.

At the front cover of this book, you can see my son and I on the amusement train.

There was another tour of my son and my husband.

My son having fun in the kids zone.

Petreon Sculpture Park, Mazotos

It is an outdoor area in the location of *Plaka*, where Savvas Koulendros creates and exhibits his magnificent sculptures. His sculptures have been created with zeal and superb craftsmanship using stones that have been taken from various areas within Cyprus. As far as his sculptures are concerned, a special place amongst them is held by the dominating *Petreos*, a tall naked man holding an ancient Greek Alb with his right arm, and a snake with his left.

Visit for: 30 minutes.

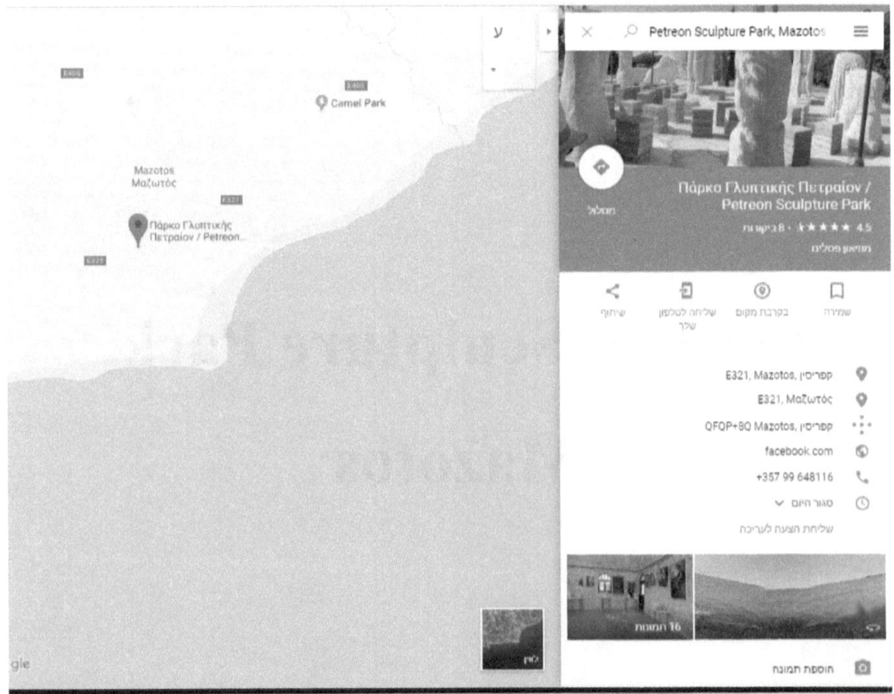

WOW Action Park

A large playground including:

The Ultimate Action Zone – For children between 4-12, this huge 3 story climbing structure includes 3 upper slides, climbs, hiding places, and countless obstacles, as well as bouncy trampolines and a super blasting cannon area.

The brave can even try the 6 meter high climbing wall!

Fantasy World – This fantastic area enclosed Under 4's World offers an unlimited fantasy, climbing and adventure play for the little ones, it includes a specially built town and a magical soft play area with little slides and obstacles. Best of all, however, it also offers respite for the adults as it is a secured area, for example only adults can open entrance gates, and is adjacent to the cafe, allowing parents to watch over their children, but still enjoy their coffee and remain carefree.

Outdoor Activities – In the summer afternoons, children are able to play outside in our lovely exterior garden area, and during weekends, we reopen our obstacle course inflatable. Our extreme 4 meter high rope course is also opened for children to test their skills and overcome a fear of heights.

Opening Hours

Tuesday – Sunday: 10:00 a.m. to 10:00 p.m.
Monday CLOSED (excluding public and school holidays)

Rates

Entrance: €4.90

Children under 1 year old and over 12 years old: FREE

Socks: €1.10

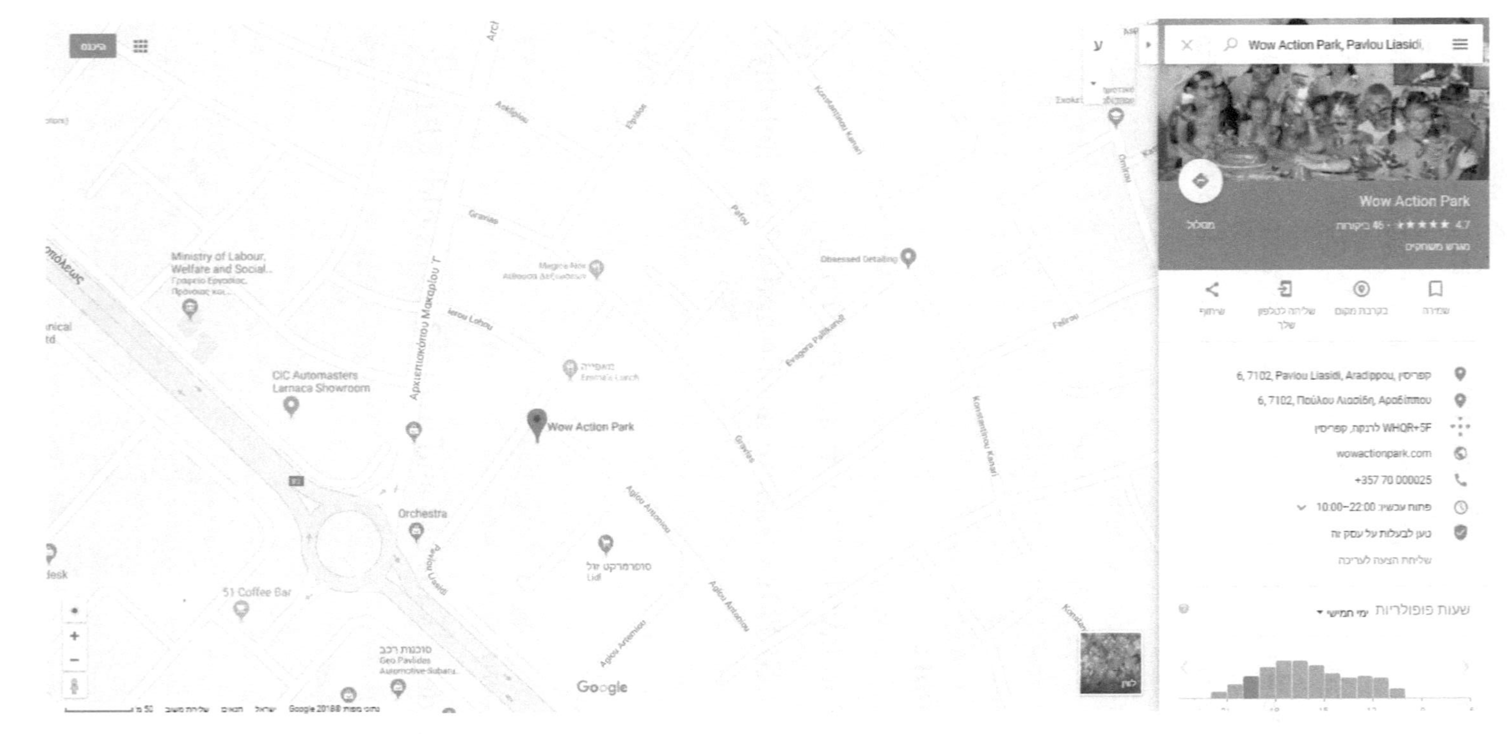

Wow Action Park, Pavlou Liasidi.
Wow Action Park
4.7 ★★★★★ · 46 ביקורות
מגרש משחקים
משחק
שיתוף
שמירה
בקרבת מקום
שליחה לטלפון שלך
6, 7102, Pavlou Liasidi, Aradippou, קפריסין
6, 7102, Πούλου Λιασίδη, Αραδίππου
WHQR+5F לרנקה, קפריסין
wowactionpark.com
+357 70 000025
פתוח עכשיו: 10:00–22:00
טען לבעלות על עסק זה
שליחת הצעה לעריכה
שעות פופולריות ימי חמישי
Ministry of Labour,
Welfare and Social..
Γραφείο Εργασίας,
Πρόνοιας και...
CIC Automasters
Larnaca Showroom
Wow Action Park
Αρχιεπισκόπου Μακαρίου Γ
Orchestra
51 Coffee Bar
סוכנות רכב
Geo Pavlides
Automotive-Subaru..
Obsessed Detailing
Pafou
Graviap
Evagora Pallikaridi
Agiou Antoniou
Agiou Antoniou
Agiou Artemiou
סופרמרקט של Lidl
Konstantinou Kanari
Konstantinou Kanari
Google
Google 2018

K Max Entertainment Centre

A little train that goes around a chocolate volcano, bowling, playground area, you are also able to see a movie with your kids. I do, however, think that it is best to take the child there if he or she is past 5 years old. Any age before that, they are usually afraid of the dark and should not be eating popcorn, it wouldn't be a healthy experience for them. Link for buying tickets: http://www.kcineplex.com/en/kids-corner/larnaka

K Cineplex Larnaca, קפריסין
K Cineplex Larnaca
4.1 ★★★★☆ · 34 ביקורות
בית קולנוע
מסלול
שיתוף
שליחה לטלפון שלך
בקרבת מקום
שמירה
Pelloponisou Potamou Indou 1 Larnaca CY, Larnaca 6042, קפריסין
WJ83+C5 לתנקה, קפריסין
kcineplex.com
+357 24 819022
שליחת הצעה לעריכה
שעות פופולריות ימי חמישי
Nikou and Despoinas Pattichi
K Cineplex Larnaca
Best Look Clothing
Apostolos Andreas
Alphamega Kamares
Giorgou Christodoulidi
AquaGym
חדר כושר
Quality Driven Tyres
Hadjipanagis Nicholas
חנות צמיגים
KFC
מסעדת עוף
PERSEAS bakery
מאפייה
Alphamega Kamares
סופרמרקט
Cyprus Car Hire
השכרת רכב
Δροσιά-Ακρόπολη-Καλογερά
423
Google

The Village Zygi

Located about 40 km from Larnaka, in between Larnaka, Lefkosia, and Lemesos, Zygi is famous on the island for its fishing shelter and fresh fish restaurants, and is build on the beach at an altitude of 8 metres. The village can be reached by following the direction from Larnaka.

The village got it's name from the Greek word *zygizo*, meaning *weigh*, as locust-bean exporters brought the beans to Zygi to be weighed and delivered to the storehouses.

Zygi's main attraction is its fishing shelter, which is surrounded by good quality fish taverns, many of which have children's facilities and attract diners from all over the island. This picturesque fishing shelter is popular for a stroll after a meal, whilst visitors can also take a traditional fishing trip, where fishermen tell tales of the sea as they demonstrate the old fishing methods.

Every year, on September 17, a festival is held in honor of *Agios (Saint) Eracledios*, whose quaint church is located on the edge of the community. The church is also believed to originally have been built at around 1800, by immigrants from Asia Minor, who settled in the area as confirmed by the graves found at the nearby cemetery.

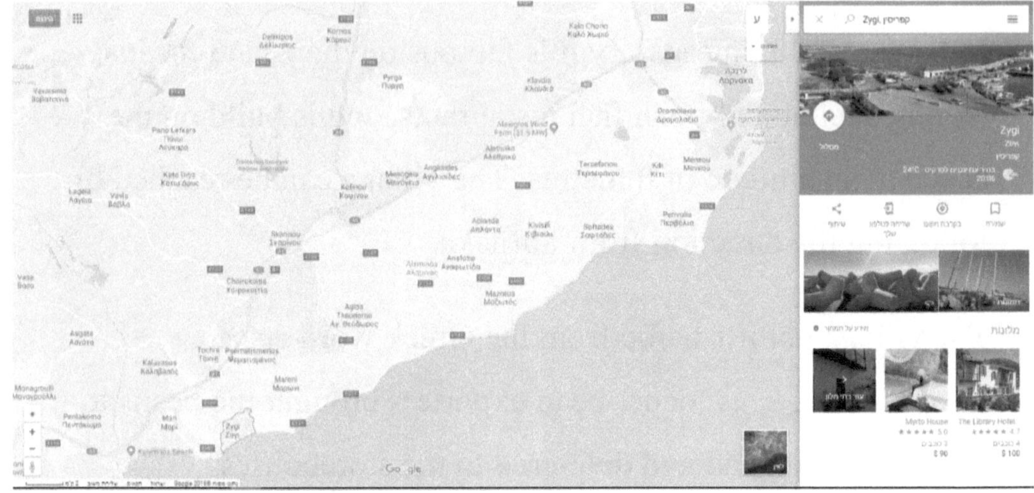

We had fun! We will return! I hope that you will have as much
as fun as we did.